About the Author

Regina Wallmark is a Business Woman with experience from many perspectives. She has a master degree within business with a major within Leadership and Finance. We all take inspiration from leaders in our lives, from childhood to adulthood. This is her second book and the first one is called *Structure is Key to Success,* there she has shared the need for anyone to take care of themselves and challenge themselves to be able to succeed as a business leader and in their career or private life. To use daily strategies to become very efficient is a smart move.

Design your Leadership Style

Regina Wallmark

Design your Leadership Style

Olympia Publishers
London

www.olympiapublishers.com
OLYMPIA PAPERBACK EDITION

Copyright © Regina Wallmark 2023

The right of Regina Wallmark to be identified as author of
this work has been asserted in accordance with sections 77 and 78 of
the Copyright, Designs and Patents Act 1988.

All Rights Reserved

No reproduction, copy or transmission of this publication
may be made without written permission.
No paragraph of this publication may be reproduced,
copied or transmitted save with the written permission of the publisher,
or in accordance with the provisions
of the Copyright Act 1956 (as amended).

Any person who commits any unauthorised act in relation to
this publication may be liable to criminal
prosecution and civil claims for damage.

A CIP catalogue record for this title is
available from the British Library.

ISBN: 978-1-80439-575-2

This is a work of fiction.
Names, characters, places and incidents originate from the writer's
imagination. Any resemblance to actual persons, living or dead, is
purely coincidental.

First Published in 2023

Olympia Publishers
Tallis House
2 Tallis Street
London
EC4Y 0AB

Printed in Great Britain

A Position of Trust

Early in our life we shape our identity with different role models that we choose to both adapt to and to imitate or take inspiration from. Teenagers often try different styles to find where they belong, a new or old culture to belong to. It is said that we are social creatures that need to feel a sense of belongingness to something. Recent studies even say that we are like the five closest people we associate with in life so throughout our life we adapt to the social circle we are in. We shape our behavior and our values consciously and unconsciously. We automatically collect information and save insights from different experiences during our life.

Superior Requirements
We look up to our boss at work and have expectations upon that boss. We often talk about our boss as either a good one or a bad one depending on their behavior. We seldom excuse a boss for bad behavior or mistakes, we excuse ourselves, even if it was our fault and take for granted that others believe us when we do that. Perhaps it was both of our faults but we blame the boss as superior in what to expect from them.

In my early career, first as an intern and later as an employee at a Swedish Bank, I came to work with one of the first bosses that has inspired me. He was very good at inspiring others and really brought the joy to work. Everyone had a very good time together and he really built a good team spirit.

I still remember when he gave me the assignment to get the archive of the bank's loans to customers in order when I had some time over. I was obviously very good at structure already then. This was the late '80s and I was twenty-two years old. In a smart way he made everyone "the boss" over different assignments, small and bigger assignments. The key here is that my actions made a huge difference of the outcome for everyone.

He said to me: "Now you are the boss of this archive, you are in charge, you can make it in what order you want to as long as you can explain to us how it is organized." He smiled and left me feeling very inspired and happy for the assignment. This was a brilliant way to both motivate and encourage me to do my very best. He also thanked me at the coffee break in front of everyone for a very good job. Very smart, and this I still remember and have been inspired by.

There was an open position at the bank that came up as an opportunity. I had a short term contract employment. I applied and the boss said at the coffee break: "We have to think about the bank's future need of executives so we will hire a man for this position."

I instantly replied: "But why can't a woman be a future executive at the bank?" He looked at me and didn't answer and continued to describe that they had a man in mind for the job. Nobody else said anything. I got really upset about this and decided to get a higher education but that took me a few years because I married and had two children a couple of years later. With my master degree I decided not to go back to the bank world since women were put at the front desk with or without a higher education, but men were put on the career ladder with or without a higher education. After my master degree within business 2003 I started to work within audit.

Business leaders communicate values consciously and unconsciously. What they say, how they say it, and how they act send important messages of the values within the company. Business leaders set the example and create the culture.

Business leaders have responsibilities over employees according to similar laws internationally. How people are treated even by other employees while interacting with each other is a responsibility for business leaders within companies. Law suits can even arise against companies from employees or unions, according to the s.k. principal employer responsibility.

We take for granted that business leaders set the example and we behave like they do. We even go so far as to adapt to the culture we work within and begin to share these values if we can't change them, or we leave the company for good. Words of values at companies are important and can be the guidance of behavior for everyone.

Words of Value

To shape preferred behavior at work words of value are something that is commonly used within companies. There can be signs or paintings on the wall close to the entrance or the coffee machine so everyone gets the reminder of these chosen words.

It's important that the employees are a part of painting the picture so to speak so the words of value are understood. It's also important that it feels like they are created together and not put up by others. Workshops in smaller groups are good to have to interact and come up with a set of rules for behavior. What is accepted and what is unaccepted behavior. These discussions are an input that can be taken into consideration when the words of value are created, together with some representatives from the employers together with the leadership team.

Select three or five words of value, not too many and not too much text to read. Explain why these words have been chosen and what they mean, the definition is important so people don't have to guess or misunderstand. Of course a set of words can be taken into consideration when a project like this is started to speed up the process, but keep these words secret for a while and let the groups be a part of the process. Either better words will come out of this or if it is the same words you know that these words really are the right ones. Don't make this process too long and bureaucratic. Prepare for the process in parallel with the group discussions at the executive level to get the leaders within the company prepared and well educated about the importance of accepted behavior.

According to decades of different science we know that we interact and create our culture together. And the business leader is a key figure in this process. If business leaders neglect the process to set up spoken guidelines there will be other persons who create the culture and the values. Business leaders give their approval to the culture either consciously or unconsciously.

There is accepted and unaccepted behavior everywhere where there are people. Every person influences the culture in a bad or a good way. Without words of value we come up with our own unspoken words of value and we even approve or disapprove behaviors automatically. Children need and seek guidance of accepted behavior and some seek it more than others and try to challenge the rules of conduct. Teenagers try to break free from their parents and want more freedom and want to set up the rules for themselves. At work some people even can take the initiative to come up with rules and force others to adapt to these rules with different tactics.

Therefore it's important to have known and spoken sets of rules for guidance on how to interact and behave towards each other at work. This ought to be the case for children throughout their school years, starting at kindergarten to my point of view. This is too important to leave in the hands of personal opinions or lack of guidance from school personnel.

Like for children some adults find these rules of conduct to be important for their safety, others take them for granted as common sense. When different behavior occurs some get surprised, upset or disappointed when values are broken, unspoken values or expected values. To avoid misunderstanding, disappointment, and mistakes, I really recommend to set up framed written words of values at work and at school and kindergarten too, even at home as a family project. We have mutual obligations towards each other's as educated humans.

Over ten years ago, approximately in 2008, I started to work at the Swedish Tax Authority within audit. We were a hundred employees and I was among the ten newly employed. The office was new and located in a new city for everyone due to a centralization project. This meant that there was a new culture to be created together by the hundred employees and five bosses. To start with I and the other new ones within the ten newly employed went into the lunch room, had coffee and were welcomed by the five bosses and went on a short-guided tour at the office and thereafter guided to our desk and got a password and email address to start up our computer and start our first assignment – the online education as new employees at this Swedish authority. The education with headphones took two days to complete.

Much of the education was about conduct and words of values within the organization and I was very impressed by how modern this was, back in 2008, and what an exceptional example for the whole society to take after. I felt very welcomed and I really loved being a part of this fantastic work place with all the colleagues and I thought that these words of conduct were so beautiful and common sense.

We have to remember that interacting together with different backgrounds and different circumstances is at hand. Some have a bad day and some have the best day since a long time ago. We interact and we share the same room so to speak, the same sequence of time together, here and now when we interact. We share our life together for a while to put it a bit philosophically. At work we share our lives for quite some time each week, right? We are on different paths, have different goals, some want to retire, others want to make a career, others just want to go home.

To have clear and set words of value internally and externally is a very smart move to start with in an introduction of new employees. There will always be some employees who try to do as they always have done their own way but new employees who get a smart introduction will just smile to such behavior and will know that this is not the behavior that is the case here anymore. This can be a move from the employer to put pressure on those who don't accept the spoken approved behavior.

The flip side of this is that the employer puts the pressure of the needed change on the shoulders of new employees instead of dealing with it directly themselves. This indirect tactic from employers get newcomers out in the organization with the unspoken mission to be the change. This unspoken tactic can be a way to try to make "oldies" within the organization either adapt to the new values or quit and leave the company.

New employees are often very careful and interested to live up to the employer's expectations to keep the job and to excel within it. New employees have the incitement to put down some effort and to be well spoken of, they are building their reputation consciously and unconsciously.

How to Manage Change

Depending on if there are difficult people at the workplace that have had bad behavior without any consequences to make it right, this can cause conflicts or pressure. If bad behavior or unaccepted behavior is neglected by the business leaders or a boss it can even be dangerous. If there is a weak leadership at hand, informal leaders will create a culture of their own and a social circle that supports it.

The problem to change a culture is that people from the "old culture" adapt differently and some even work against it or question it openly and cause a lot of tension that even has a negative effect on the productivity within the company. Uncertainty about how things will look in the future is a challenge that people react very differently to.

Some even don't understand the change and find culture as something abstract and perhaps not even important. The insight of how we act, say and do at work is the culture and everyone's responsibility. To do everything the same way as we always have done is the same thing as trying to stop time and not develop the company towards changed expectations both from the society and from the market.

I once heard the comment at a large and well-known company in Sweden: "I am not against change if I know that the outcome will be better." This is a comment of decision making from an employee, that he or she will determine if the change is successful or not. Of course everyone is entitled to a point of view but the need to change has to be taken into consideration. Why the change is needed is of course crucial to explain and it has to be the honest version because people can become suspicious otherwise and they really have the right to know why to my opinion.

To not say the truth about the needed change is not a good idea because when the words get out that the real reason was something else everyone will feel used and deceived and the productivity of that is deadly to a company. Other versions will of course arise as rumors too within the company and therefore it is better to say from the beginning of a change project why the change is needed and it shall come from the highest executive within the company.

Allow questions or make smaller groups directly after the information and encourage to contribute with ideas to the change, how to do the change. A framework of rules how to structure or how to make the change is good to involve employees within small groups. Even if they don't have any ideas, they will be a part of the important reactions and feel involved in the process of change and they will know what is happening. This builds trust and engagement for the company.

Subject	Responsible	Delegated	Responsible	Implementation
Company Vision	Management team	Employees divided into small groups	Management team	Management team
[M]anagement (Mgmt) meeting [ab]out Company's [v]ision, decision [m]aking and [do]cumentation [ab]out chosen [v]ision.	Meeting with Employees about the Company's Vision. Workshop with Employees in small groups with suggestions of Words of Values, 3-5 words. Documentation back to Mgmt same day.	Follow up Mgmt meeting same day for an overview. Documentation and analysis day 2-4 by Mgmt representative. Presentation day 5 to Mgmt for review and reflection about choice of words of value according to the Company's Vision. Suggestion about 3-5 words.	Day 8 Presentation & Follow up to the Employees as a presentation about the work process and explanations why these words have been chosen and the definition of the words why they harmonize with the Company's Vision.	Chosen words off to artist who will make paintings about the words with a very short deadline and then back to hang up well seen by everyone at work, near the entrance when you come in and at the coffee machine.
[D]ocumentation is [sm]art to make not [so] burdensome to [cr]eate and to later [re]ad. Make an [in]dex about the [su]bject of the [ch]ange, in this case [w]e have illustrated [th]e creation of a [Co]mpany's Words [of] Values. Save an [eff]ective and useful [do]cumentation.	With other changes use this tactic similarly to get people involved. Of course projects can take months but try not to make the projects too long so people get tired of being in transit to change too long without getting there and seeing the benefit of it.	Day 6 meeting with HR, union and some employee representatives with input and opinions and a chosen artist or illustrator with his or her perspective. Day 7 Mgmt meeting vote for 3-5 words of Value matching the Vision of the Company.	Thank you to everyone involved. Cake or sandwiches as a day to celebrate. Temporary signs with the chosen words put up by the coffee machine.	Follow up meeting by Mgmt when the paintings have arrived. Implemented into follow up meetings with personel a few times a year. Words of values implemented into the organisation and behavior through examples by managers and others and part of the yearly individual talks.

Strong voices as a result of the changes are not a bad thing, let them say what they want to say, listen and confirm that you hear what they are saying and take it into consideration. This is an important way to show and gain respect that will set the value of the change from the start. People deal very differently with uncertainty and to really listen to all sorts of voices about the change will actually speed up the process towards the change because you show this respect.

Document the process and the input from the employees. A good idea is to make room for written suggestions if some may not want to say the suggestions or their worries out loud. Document this in the process and remember to make a follow up on how to solve these worries and communicate the chosen way to proceed with the change.

With these follow up meetings in larger groups it is very important that it take place quite near in time to the first information meeting and the small group meeting, because the employees are waiting for your feedback from their input. If you wait too long they will feel as if you don't really care or that you just did this for show and the production will of course decline a lot from this.

A follow up meeting with the next steps of the process and talking about the raised worries and how you will solve that and how to proceed is very good.

The last decades have included much change within companies and some may be really tired of all the changes. Take this into consideration. What have we learned during the previous changes? What have we gained? What was not successful? Make this analysis and communicate these insights at the starting information meeting to win time and to use the intelligence and knowledge that the company have gained during the other change projects. And reply to the crucial question: Why is another change needed?

Here we understand the importance of a good and effective documentation of the previous change projects so no insights or knowledge gained are lost if a key person leaves the company. A quite short and well- structured written analysis of previous changes is important. Not too long and time consuming both to write and for others to read who have the responsibility of old and new change projects. A shorter version that is communicated to all employees is also good to have within this analysis so we know what has been communicated internally and externally and what has not been communicated.

The point here is both to really learn about previous change projects and to realize that there are people within the organization that have gone through many changes and question why to h a v e another change. This is also a strong argument towards speeding up the time of change. The feeling of always being in a change mode is challenging and few appreciate it. To divide, change projects into three phases is a good idea and the amount of time that it will take.

Within large projects celebrate each phase with the employees and talk about the gains and how you have solved the problems together along the way. Celebrate with some cakes or a lunch, because everyone appreciates an occasion to celebrate progress and will talk about this milestone outside the company too.

Its a milestone to reach the next level of change within your company and it gives you and everyone else an important feeling of accomplishment that gives energy to continue and even some joy. Don't underestimate this.

Of course, projects can take months but try not to make the projects too long so people get tired of being in transit for change for too long without getting there and seeing the benefit of it.

Some Governance Through History

Just a brief overview of some forms of government throughout history is interesting. The point is to identify different leadership traits, so here we go.

- **Anarchy** means that there is no government at hand who have the power over people. One conclusion can be that there is a lack of trust from the people to support a leader, or a leader lacks the leadership needed for people to support them.
- **Aristocracy** means that wealthy nobles have the power over people.
- **Capitalism** is driven by private ownership with open competition and a free market economy.
- **Colonialism** is when another country's rules crosses borders and it acts as superior to implement its values and beliefs into another country.
- **Communism** is driven by public ownership and an absence of class divisions.
- **Democracy** means that the people are given the power and choose their leadership.
- **Federalism** combines and divides powers between centralized federal authority states or territories.
- **Feudalism** is based on land ownership, nobility or military obligation and separate classes such as nobles, clergy and peasants and it is impossible to get opportunities if you

belong to the wrong class.

- **Kleptocracy** is power through corruption and/or theft.
- **Dictatorship** is absolute power in the hands of a single authority figure usually connected to a military structure.
- **Monarchy** is absolute power and authority to members of a royal bloodline.
- **Oligarchy** is a set of groups that rule a nation based on their wealth, race or heredity. Aristocratic and plutocratic can be viewed as oligarchy.
- **Plutocracy** is power determined by wealth.
- **Socialism** means that the people share ownership and equal distribution of resources, another view is a free market capitalism together with a public administration.
- **Totalitarianism** is when a ruling party recognizes no limitations of power and demands total control.
- **Tribalism** means an absence of a central authority and locally governance is in the hands of warlords or patriarchs.

From the different governance ideologies there can of course be a combination of different leadership styles in each one of these ideologies.

Leadership style is of course influenced by the culture and history.

What Have we Learned from History

From the history we can say that good intentions d o n't always get a great outcome and we sometimes get really surprised that bad intentions get so much power. We need to learn from the history, we keep on learning and seem to never get enough about this important subject.

Elitism is a belief of leadership by an elite. Suspicion about injustice has easily been raised. Even within organizations critical voices are raised when someone is chosen for a leader or on the leadership ladder just based on wealth, family belonging or inner circle. Elitism also causes criticism that the norm is expected for everyone and leaves people less fortunate behind.

About labeling it is important to not narrow the sight with anger and stop listening, it's better to really talk about what this word means to share the same understanding. What does this word mean to you? What does it mean to me? What negative versus positive aspects do you associate with elitism? If you are against it, does it mean that you want anarchy? If you prefer it, does it mean that you want dictatorship? Hopefully not. Listen to understand the other one's standpoint and then come with your perspective. I will come back to this later.

To avoid reinventing the wheel or historical disasters as a leader it is important to study different leaders as either inspiration or as a warning. Choose what and who to get influenced by, ancient Kings, entrepreneurs, athletes and politicians. Alexander the Great is said to be the inspiration for the word strategy – Greek meaning generalship. Strategy is a foundation within the field of leadership. To pick pieces from the history is very interesting and a responsible way to act, to really contribute to progress in leadership. How to reach higher levels as a leader is another important aspect.

Within companies starting at the bottom and to work your way up has been a time-consuming way to reach higher positions within a company. On the other hand much information is gained with a hands- on experience throughout a company. In recent years some paid internships or programs for new employees have been implemented within large companies for new employees to get this experience. On the other hand younger employees are not as interested to stay with a company as earlier generations.

In recent years experienced business leaders have had to step aside for younger business leaders with the remark that new leaders are needed and we want to leave outdated values behind us. This is an important mark that your leadership style needs to adapt to time and modern expectations if you want to keep the job or change to another interesting assignment.

The same with political leaders, they get outdated or are perhaps promoted as outdated with the media's help. Today news travels fast through social media and quotes can raise quickly to international proportions. Therefore, it is obviously a need for shared values and expectations upon leaders, both political and within companies. Values have in the last f e w years become international expectations like never before thanks to social media. It speeds things up and some cultures have decades to catch up with and they want it now. People want freedom of speech and freedom of choice.

It's a good thing when good values of respect and equality are spread as expectations throughout the world. But it also requires a bold leadership to take a stand against bad things such as trafficking, violence and fraud or money laundering. The market is international and we can therefore expect that the world kind of gets smaller and we both get the good and the bad of it. The important thing is to be aware of the possible threats to our companies. To be aware of threats and to have skilled employees and manager teams is important.

To have the right people round you with right values can never be underestimated.

We will now go deeper into a characteristics perspective of leadership.

Some Characteristics of Leaders

There are some classical leadership styles that it is of interest to discuss here.

Autocratic leadership means that one person controls all the decisions and take very little input from other group members. **Autocratic leaders** make choices or decisions based on their own beliefs and do not involve others for their suggestion, advice or second opinion.

Laissez-faire leadership, on the other hand, is a type that historically has been viewed as a weaker leadership style. In recent years it has been given the name **delegative leadership** and can have its advantages. But to leave the decision making to others can result in problems and imbalance if there are constant compromises that turn things upside down and decisions are changed. This can lead to confusion and doubt within the company.

Strategic leadership style refers to a manager's potential to express a strategic vision for the organization, or a part of the organization, and to motivate and persuade others to acquire that vision. That can be very time consuming and very expensive for a company that really needs to change. The key here is to speed the process up to be effective to my point of view.

When designing your leadership style you can write down pros and cons about each of these leadership styles and what situations they may work in or not in companies today.

This is not about acting like a stereotype, that is to minimize this topic. Knowledge about these leadership styles will help you in different situations because you can remind yourself how the different classical leadership styles would handle the situation.

For me working within international companies the past six years as an interim consultant this is very interesting. At one company I was the representative from the financial department as a division controller with colleagues round the world meeting up virtually even before Covid-19. To be a part of the management team together with different cultures' view of leadership is very interesting. The division president was called "The American" after the weekly meeting that had different levels of adrenaline to it and many felt the need to talk about him at the next meeting without him.

I defended him and said once that "he expects us to use our brains that's all, he really believes that we can do it together, and when we fail, he shows his disappointment and worry." I also helped out to sort the terrain and remind the managers about different things to both be there present for them and to show compassion and encouragement within these projects, and the skill to put it all together with excellence, and we did.

He hung up and left one meeting because everyone was not prepared enough, he was wasting his time, he said. This leadership style can foster a climate where you hesitate to contribute with your thoughts freely. A meeting culture where you are prepared is of course important but you don't want to cause unnecessary tension. It is better to organize meetings with a time for thoughts to contribute with and the time to prepare instead of acting on a rush from the whole team that was the case here.

Perhaps, it was unclear what was expected of each one of the managers. That is something to really take into consideration. The job descriptions are good for managers to know each other so they see everyone's contribution to the whole picture. It is also a good idea to have follow-up meetings on what went wrong and why and see where it can be fixed and learn from and perhaps adjust strategies or even job descriptions. Learn to become better together is a smart move and that ties teams together.

To pretend that all is good and just go with a good mood attitude on the next meeting is just to swipe it all under the rug so to speak. The tension remains and no-one can talk about it or sort it out. A recap is important. Say how you want it to be done and acknowledge the time needed for it.

A Laissez-faire leader is the opposite to an Autocratic leader. These opposites can be described very roughly that a Laissez-faire leader changes his standpoint perhaps many times along the way while an Autocratic leader never changes his or her mind or even listens to input or criticism.

To make decisions and take responsibility for the decisions is one thing. To prepare and take into consideration others' view points and experience before making a decision is a completely different thing. You can call off a meeting because people are not prepared or something else because perhaps you are wasting time with a meeting that is leading nowhere. But then follow up with guidelines or a short agenda to what you expect out of the meetings in the future. No blaming, just facts and a good tone.

One problem with a leader that keeps changing decisions or not following decisions is that it communicates uncertainty and ruins trust and in the long run perhaps an entire company.

The recent years' change or development into a s.k. **delegative leadership** is of course interesting and modern. To believe in employees is a good thing that makes people prosper within organizations. Guidelines and job descriptions are important and good to review and update to learn along the way. It is good because people feel that they are taken into consideration and that what they contribute with really matters; we all want to make a difference and job fulfillment is a basic human need. It is though important to keep a structure within the culture so it doesn't tip over to be a Laissez-faire leadership where managers fails to make decisions and to take responsibility for the decisions made.

Personality traits are of course part of our leadership style. Leadership is much about how you view other people. Your intentions or purpose are also the foundation of your leadership style that you create both consciously and unconsciously. Of course your upbringing is a factor of influence for your leadership style. Opportunities or lack of opportunities along the way, and even setbacks, either fuels or limits your progress as a leader.

Masculine & Feminine Leadership

One of my final major courses within leadership at D level was an international student exchange course – Leadership and Gender. The topic was much about what a masculine versus a feminine leadership style is, and the differences. This doesn't mean what sex you belong to because men can have more of a feminine leadership style and women can have a masculine leadership style.

Cultural Differences
In Sweden I for instance had the possibility to take my master degree within business in my hometown when my two boys started school. Combining children and a family life with college studies is not an option everywhere in the world. When I studied the Leadership and Gender course there were some students from India and one of them was a woman. The men explained that she only had the opportunity to study at the university because she came from a wealthy family. To study at a university was not impossible for not wealthy men, but impossible for not wealthy women. Opportunities for women are not the same everywhere as we know.

In recent years the world has become more internationalized since many move to other continents and cultures to have a career. Here in Stockholm it is very internationalized and I like that a lot. Especially within large international companies you can move within the company to different countries and make a career. That means that different cultural backgrounds interact within the same "four walls" at many companies round the world.

A culture is both about your origin or background that you grew up in and the culture at school. A culture does also exist within companies, both locally and internationally, for international companies. To have possibilities to move across the world creates an international atmosphere and culture as a mixture of influence from different backgrounds and experiences.

Historical masculine leadership traits are still viewed by many as the requirements for a good leader. Traits such as being authoritative, taking up much space, outgoing, easy to express themselves, dominant, bulldozing, competitive, physically strong and so on has been taken for granted and been pictured as a man. A leader has historically been seen as a strong warrior for a battlefield and some even view an argument as a battlefield.

A feminine leadership style is often described as more about including others in the decision-making process and more natural to involve employees at any level within a company.

A masculine leadership culture has often been about a mans' club, an inner circle bullet proof so that no information gets out whatsoever to the company. The silent treatment has its roots here. It gives a feeling of being superior that no information whatsoever gets out and through the company as if thinking or using the brain is something that no-one else should bother with. This is a foundation for gossip and talking behind people's back since information travels anyway and misunderstanding can be very expensive and foolish if people start to guess.

Of course there are confidential topics but to have an inclusive attitude and make reviews and discuss that with smaller groups is a good way to open up and not be so old fashioned and prestigious.

A leadership with only men can have a cultural reason or educational reason, as for instance engineers that historically have been mostly men who studied, but it doesn't have to mean that there is no influence or input from the company. It is important that it is a dialogue where insights, knowledge and experience are moving throughout the company. No-one likes monologues and it is not beneficial for a company because it kind of kills engagement and motivation. To talk above the heads of other people is a superior attitude and that shuts down communication and the company loses much knowledge and insights.

To listen to what other people have to say is not a weakness or does not mean that you are losing power, it means that you show respect and realize that there is much knowledge within the company. A superior "to know it all" attitude can result in much knowledge being lost.

To allocate women or representatives from minority groups by quotas into leadership teams still requires an inclusive attitude to really work. And to really welcome the knowledge, insights and experiences from these persons. A leadership team can be divided into smaller groups, like within politics with supporters that take turns on how they vote on each other's favorite topics or agendas. Here again prestige is not for the good of the company. Listen and take into consideration what is being said instead of who says it.

Entrepreneurs often have a more casual culture and even international entrepreneurial companies can have a family feeling to them and still be masculine.

Competition
I worked temporarily as a finance manager a few years ago part time at an international company with small administration offices in twenty-five countries. The company had a strong feeling of family ties within the company from the owners of the company and the managing directors, finance directors, and others at high levels. It was a feeling of being included and we were often even told the gratitude that everyone's work contributed much to the company. It was a spoken culture where everyone was seen as a part of a family.

There was though some prestige between some of the coworkers and to my opinion it had to do partly because of the brand's reputation and long history that was impressive. The other part I identified was about not giving women the same opportunities to reach a higher position as a leader within the company. Most at manager level and higher positions were men. The culture since the '50s has kind of stuck to the company. An entrepreneurial culture tends to be less flexible to change since the founder sets the culture and has to do much to change it.

Just to lean on the history of '50s the achievements thanks to the founder can make the culture get stuck in some values. The culture is built round the founder's family and a history of many men in managerial positions fosters a competitive culture between women when younger women start within the company and get promoted.

I recognize that same behavior from when I started my career at a bank in Sweden and worked at their different small offices, but that was thirty years ago. Especially among women there were competitive destructive attitudes towards women who really got the chance to become a manager. Those who didn't become managers or hadn't seen that opportunity in their career talked behind the backs of those who did. Back then I learned the meaning of – " If I haven't had that chance in my career, I will not support any other women who will" – Attitude. And the saying that it is lonely at the top for sure was applicable here.

Within this bank in Sweden some women in their 50s were given the manager role back then and I knew some of them and they said the same, that there was jealousy or envy. I have seen this at other companies through my whole career so it still exists today.

I also recognize this from a large company in Sweden that I worked at a few years ago. Younger women of similar ages at higher positions were talked about in a negative way among many women in lower positions.

Attitudes really show and disappointment is something that can be dealt with personally. To make a strong come back is possible if you have a good strategy and develop good leadership skills. Of course there is competition to walk the career ladder, the question is how you deal with it.

There is of course competition between men, and always has been. In the 70's women came to be interested in making a career and adopted masculine behavior to get where they wanted, or w h e r e accepted to these positions for their masculine behavior since these skills were the norm for leadership.

Competition is something that is good to use on yourself, to become better and even more skilled. Use it as a motivation factor to excel within what you do. Work on your leadership style and don't turn into someone you are not. Show your skills with your leadership style in your everyday life and you will be the change and contribute to a healthy leadership development in your culture because we all influence the culture that we are in.

Expected Behavior
Depending on our cultural background and our insights along the way we have expectations of leadership. Within a company this can mean many different perspectives. To view women as intellectually weaker or less intelligent is an outdated belief and not right. To expect s.k. historically masculine traits for leadership is also outdated and not right. And to expect physical strength, a pushy and bulldozing attitude in leadership is not suitable for anyone in a modern society. To frighten people in to submissive behavior is dictatorship and destructive behavior.

In Sweden there has been a movement against "The Macho Culture" with the twisted image about how men are to behave, expectations that have many touchpoints from the entertainment industry. Men are seen as strong and defensive warriors and if you can't identify with that you are neither a leader or a man. "The Macho Culture" has connections with abuse, drugs and other addictions. To speak up and have opinions in a non-violent and non-abusive way is to master the skill of communication, we will get into this soon.

Being masculine is not the same as being violent and aggressive. Being violent and aggressive is not a question of gender and it destroys everything in its way, even the persons inner being, rather than contributing to progress. These traits are not the skills of leadership either, they're more like rebellion and chaos.

When women got into management teams or at higher positions from the '80s and decades to follow, they were women in their late '50s and with many masculine leadership traits. Leadership is still seen by many employees as being by a man or at least someone with masculine leadership traits.

Of course you may say that it depends on what kind of company it is.

Within companies with many engineers, auditors, lawyers and other highly educated people; historically t h e r e have been few women as business leaders. Not because men have higher educations but because in these fields more men have chosen these educations.

At universities there are also cultures and of course with a history of a majority of male students' women are a minority group that is within a masculine culture. Universities I dare to say have a much longer time to adapt and change to a new culture than within companies because the market requires companies to adapt.

Students come to universities to learn and after a few years new students come into the culture that is more fixed than a company to my point of view. It is therefore very important that universities get updated cultures and values and not just stick to their history. Students and employees automatically try to influence a culture with their natural behavior and will try to change cultures because wherever there are people that interact there is change.

Students and employees will though adapt to the present culture if an effort to change the culture is not encouraged behavior or even sanctioned behavior. Within companies younger employees are an important part of change and many set the term for change to stay within the company for a few years, not accepting an old culture like previous generations have done. Within a university this is more difficult because your grades are what you need as a student so you may reason that "I will be here a few years, get my degree and then I'm out of here" – instead of working on changing an old culture.

If you view something as temporary you will not put down so much work and effort to change a culture, especially if that behavior is not an encouraged behavior. You will do your work and count down the time towards when you are out of there.

The Skill of Communication
Even within communication we have expectations, depending on our cultural background, on how a man talks and how a woman talks. We also have an opinion on what is a masculine way and a feminine way to communicate. This is crucial within leadership.

If you take a closer look at psychology about body language, first impressions, behavior, verbal expressions and other visual appearances you will find many interesting insights. We all kind of categorize people either consciously and/or unconsciously because of our culture and previous experiences in life, good and bad.

Communication is much about body language, then how you say things rather than what you say. Your appearance in style and clothes does also make a difference depending on where you are and if you know the people you are communicating with. First impressions last. To be dressed for the occasion is a way to show respect.

To try to be someone that you're not will not be successful anywhere and you will feel like you have betrayed yourself. It's important that you stay true to yourself and your values. That said you need to cultivate and sharpen the skills you have.

There are expectations upon a leader and especially a new leader. A culture is something that we need to consider as something that need to develop and make people be an active part of. We influence the culture and other people and the everyday life we share at our workplace. We are a piece in the puzzle and contribute to the whole picture so to speak. What we do, say and how we act influences the company every day.

The skill of communication can be learned with our feelings in control and our mental power focused on what we want to accomplish. To really listen requires effort and to show empathy for another person is to be a human.

To speak up and have opinions in a non-violent and non-abusive way is to master the skill of communication.

There are different approaches to communication, some talk very straightforwardly and others beat about the bush more and take a detour before they get to the point. Think about what has influenced you through your career, and how it was communicated in different situations. This can be a real eyeopener to the skill of communication.

Think about when you felt that you really got through with what you wanted to say, and when you didn't. Also think about others when they really got through to you and when they didn't, much is about how they said it rather than what. This is a bit sad because we ought to think the other way that it is important what others say more than how they say it, but we get caught up with our emotions and if we get really upset we can almost stop listening and just act on our emotions. Our feelings are really something that we need to learn to control ourselves.

Feminine personality traits have historically been identified as submissive, silent, smiling and not having too much to say. But this is more about being extrovert or being introvert and not about what sex you are and not about your leadership style either.

If you are the kind of person that thinks that all have the right to be listened to, sometimes you need to interrupt or at least make the hint that you also want to say something and be a part of a discussion. Use it to show that you also are an individual that has the right to say your opinion. Some just get carried away with their feelings and take up all the space. That is better to interrupt in a good way and act towards having a part of the discussion than later being angry for not been given the chance. Say at least something at every meeting or event where that is possible, because you are doing your part in creating a culture where your opinions are appreciated and taken into consideration.

Communication includes listening and how we communicate with our body language. Performing artists look at themselves in the mirror to see their expressions, it is an important part of their job. Look at politicians and other officials and in movies. We unconsciously interpret others' body language and others interpret ours. To look at yourself in the mirror is something I took up in my first book, *Structure is Key to Success*. This is a very good way to encourage yourself to choose your attitude and approach. You are what you think of yourself, and it shows.

This is not to be done in a theatrical way, you are you

and you have your ways to express yourself both physically and verbally. But if you feel that you are not getting through it is a good idea to sharpen your communication skills and see if you can deliver your opinions in another way to get really heard and understood. Challenge yourself to master the skills of communication better and you will improve your influence wherever you go in life. And give everyone else the gesture of listening to what they have to say and you will gain respect.

The Extinction of Femininity

An explosive topic to discuss is femininity. Throughout history there have been so many comments and expectations on how a woman should look, act and behave. Today there are no stereotypes but still there is a lot of argument about how women should look and not. The thing is that all want the right to decide themselves as everyone should, but that also means within this topic that everybody else also has that right.

Feminists have been accused of being haters of men just because they speak up for equal rights between all sexes. Forget that definition once and for all. To have equal rights doesn't mean that the other part gets less rights, it means equal rights, it's not a cake as someone pointed out.

Feminism is still much about taking down the patriarchy. It's about men having a majority of influential positions and getting paid more for the same job. I for instance had a better experience and higher education when I started at the Swedish Tax Agency and I had two hundred Euro less each month in salary than a ten-years-younger man working at the same position. I pointed out this and got even less raise from the boss with the comment that I had interfered with the annual salary review. So they raised the gap between us. Are you surprised that this was one reason that I quit and left the building, this was 2010?

To be afraid that a woman might win an argument and be more intelligent is something really challenging still in the western world. Competition between sexes is really stupid and is like living in the dark ages. To take for granted that men are more suitable for business leaders' positions is completely wrong. Leadership has to do with personality traits and experience, not what sex you are.

The patriarchy is an ancient family organization form where the oldest man made all the decisions because he had the most experience of the world that they got exposed to. Often in polygamous families and a woman was very fortunate if she got many children. Some cultures still live like this today even though it ought to have been out of the history thousands of years ago to my point of view.

Today it doesn't work that way that the oldest man has all the insights to live in a modern society. I will later come in to the subject that it is often quite the opposite really, since modern society has changed so much in just the past few years so you have to stay updated.

This doesn't mean that a younger person stays updated automatically. If you want to have a modern leadership style you have to know what society we live in, you have to have the shared reality together with those whom you are responsible for as a business leader. And you need some knowledge about previous leadership styles, what good it can be used for.

I like to talk about the topic of female business leaders, that over the last decades they have been expected to have a masculine leadership style. Perhaps because it has been the notion that leadership is to be masculine.

The process of decision making has historically been viewed as a monologue where the boss knows everything by heart and his or her position involves communication downwards with instructions, not dialogues. On the contrary much can be learned with two-way communication. To be present at every level within the company makes the communication more spontaneous, and in the moment, i n s i g h t s are easier taken into consideration.

Nowadays communication privately on social media is much about asking questions. Perhaps it is because the online marketing is much about asking question to customers. For instance to ask "what do you think about this?" is an open question to get people engaged in a dialogue and find out more, to get important insights about your customers.

To communicate with statements like "this is the solution to this problem" is not that appreciated. People want to feel involved and asked for their opinion and feel that they make their own decisions. This is the case in their private life. This is the case with customers too.

If this will be the case within companies a business leader will need the communication skills and insights to get decisions implemented. It is historically viewed as a feminine trait to ask before you act to have a softer side and include others in your decision making. It is viewed as a masculine trait to just do without asking for permission or opinions.

People want to be involved and feel that they are taken into consideration. To open up to dialogues is a more feminine leadership style and it can be done effectively. Listen and confirm that you understand what you heard by replying t o what they have said in your own words. Wait for a confirmation "yes" that you have understood. Take it into consideration, suggest the strategy and wait for input, and then decide. It doesn't have to be more bureaucratic that this.

If companies view this as too time consuming it might mean that masculine leadership styles will continue to be preferred rather than feminine softer traits. I hope that business leaders will appreciate the positive affects of an inclusive culture where mutual respect for opinions and influence is the way to do it. I think it is to go backwards if we have patriarchies with women or men with masculine oppressive behavior anywhere within our society.

Human Rights

The United Nations Declaration of Human Rights was adopted in 1948 and is described as rights that all human beings inherit worldwide. Human rights means that regardless of race, sex, nationality, ethnicity, language, religion, or any other status you have the same rights. This includes the right to life and liberty, freedom from slavery and torture, freedom of opinion and expression, the right to work and education, and more. Everyone is entitled to these rights, without discrimination, worldwide.

The deep meaning in these rights is much about integrity, to respect everyone's right to make choices in life and the right to the same value as a human being. This has not been accomplished throughout the world despite much effort. One has to wonder why because they really are beautiful and basic rights that ought to be something that is taken for granted.

The problem is that rich countries have exploited poor countries. The attitude of taking advantage of other nationalities and other country's wealth to get richer has been an issue throughout history. After world war II we kind of thought that we would have learned that we all deserve the same rights and want to live in peace and harmony.

The internationalization where many large companies are based across the world has led to possibilities to work in another country across the world within the same company. And while in that company the possibility appears to make a career and change to another company within that country. The possibilities are many, to study abroad as well. This makes the world smaller so to speak and more people want to live the western lifestyle where you can decide how you want to live and not being governed by a culture at home.

The wish to decide for yourself ought to give the insight that others want to do the same. There is a mixture of all sorts of lifestyles in the western society and we can't force anyone to do anything, that is a very outdated strategy. But we still have old practices like child marriages, young girls genital mutilation, trafficking and other violent and abusive destinies.

This is the reality as we know it today and we have to raise these topics within our companies that this is exploitation of humans that is not accepted behavior to any human being. We can make charity events or contributions to well- respected organizations and inform internally and externally within our companies that we support these organizations and what they are working for. This way we raise the awareness within the company and externally as well and we can make a bigger difference than if we do nothing and just look away as if it doesn't exist.

A Call for a Modern Leadership

Power has been the drive for many to reach positions of decision making over people and assets throughout history. Many have been driven by greed and obsession to the cost of others. Extortion and corruption are something that has been an ingredient throughout history and we are all sick of it.

Gatekeepers Against Change

In smaller portions some business leaders still use similar tactics to threaten and force employees to stay back in line with outdated behavior. Some cultures within companies are stuck decades back thanks to their business leaders that work as gatekeepers against change. An imagined safety with an outdated culture is not that uncommon. The horror of losing control of something that feels familiar can be a real problem within companies. A wise thing is to make business leaders from an old culture resign and not have anything to do with development of the new culture if there are signs that they will not cooperate.

To say that you have decades of experience within a company can be an indicator that you carry on the old and not wanted culture with you. If you have been a part of a management team for over a decade and you haven't been working on developing a modern culture within the company, you are not a modern leader. Cultures need to work continuously with their culture so it really is the culture throughout the entire company. It has to be implemented in the everyday work.

Old cultures can be very rooted and the business leaders are the ones that carry the load of setting the example for the change. The new behaviors have to be safeguarded against the rooted not accepted behavior and actions are needed when these behaviors sometimes come up to the surface again by employees or business leaders.

New business leaders need to understand the old culture and what it didn't accomplish and why a new culture is what is expected. Companies are like small or big islands with people that interact and with many international companies that together create an international culture.

Internationalization
Voices a round the world call for change and equality. People aren't stupid, they spot devious tactics right away and unhealthy mistrust rises against almost everything within our society almost to the outbreak of anarchy. Violence has never solved anything, it has always caused losses and pain.

I think it is very beautifully said to *"be the change"*. It starts with you. If everyone would realize this and act accordingly, it would make a huge difference.

With the internationalization everything kind of speeds up. Cultures that have not been part of the western world have in the last decades entered into the internationalization. I visited Zhuhai in China i n 2016 and this province had been a fishing village only thirty years before, and now it was a multi-international city with only new cars and new buildings. You could spot a monk with their traditional clothing and that really almost looked photoshopped or like you were in a movie where something unexpected appeared. One generation can be the change to something entirely new. This can be something good if the intentions are good for the benefit of others and not for selfish greed or craving for power. The province where Zhuhai is located is an experiment of market economy in China.

Within a company this has to be the case, that modern values are the ones that are the culture. To show respect is something that should be mutual. We don't have to have the same opinions, but we need to be able to cooperate even if we have differences. Sometimes we need to agree that we disagree and make the best out of it. At work we do what is expected according to our work description and cooperate to the values within the company.

Internationalization means that we bring different cultural background with us and that is something we have to accept when it comes to the personal right to decide how we live our lives. But it also means that we have to respect other people's rights to choose what they decide is right for them. It doesn't mean that we need to agree, we may not understand because we are not accustomed to it. A personal decision is personal and does not involve other people.

A culture that prospers and has many different cultural backgrounds can be something really enriching when mutual respect is at hand. To discuss and listen to others' backgrounds is a good way to understand and a way to show mutual respect.

Responsibility Versus Power

To be ambitious can have a different meaning to it. The positive side is to want to become better and achieve goals. A negative meaning of the word can be that someone does whatever it takes, with no boundaries whatsoever to reach their goals in life for the sake of other people.

Power has kind of intoxicated people throughout history and within companies too. When you think about what comes with leadership you really have to realize that you are obligated to step into the shoes of responsibility. That ought to get that cocky attitude out of you and make you see that you are responsible for other people's everyday life at the company. People spend a large part of their lives at their workplace and they are entitled to be treated with respect and care. People are not machines. People are humans.

A piece of good advice: don't treat people like they are stupid, they will spot devious tactics right away and unhealthy mistrust will rise against you and spread throughout the company and eventually to your customers too.

To base your leadership style on emotions is really bad and a toxic behavior for everyone round you. We all have feelings and we are each one of us responsible for how we control our feelings. To master your feelings is the first step of self-leadership and that is crucial and an obligation you have towards other people. If you master this skill you will also have better relationships within your family and between your friends.

Again I am not talking about being a robot but to burst out in feelings of anger, bitterness, hate, and even panic will get you out of your own control. To train yourself to keep calm and to calm yourself and others close to you could even save lives in a case of emergency.

What do you think about this attitude? – "I am the one who makes all the decisions here!" Perhaps such a statement is needed if there is anarchy within a company. There is definitely a problem if you need to explain this. Decision making is about taking in information, listening to input, having dialogues, analyzing and making the decision. Who makes the decision is something that is not even a discussion and again, people are not stupid. Sometimes it is a misunderstanding of input or suggestions that comes your way.

Input and suggestions don't mean that you are questioned so don't feel threatened by discussions. A suggestion or opinions is not the same thing as taking away your power to decide on the matter. It doesn't mean that you are threatened in your position at all. If you feel threatened, listen even more and even to outbursts of anger if you have to, let them get it out how they feel. Other people might act on emotions and feel the need to say their opinion in a harsh way, perhaps because they are nervous but try to find why they have this need. Listen to what they have to say, and again repeat with your own words what they have said and ask if you have understood their point of view. Say that you will take it into consideration and say that you will come back and have a new discussion in the next day or so. Schedule a time. And be calm.

This is a good idea. The frustration from the other person has made him or her think over what they have said and you have listened to them. To wait until the next day will calm things down. It is not a bad thing if someone really needs to say what they think because perhaps they haven't ever got the chance to do that ever. If they keep doing this it is a completely different thing. That is not accepted behavior at all. You need to inform them what the tone of communication is within the company and stick to it yourself. You create the culture and it will work. You need to deal with these situations to be a business leader. You are reachable and reasonable, you listen and comment, you show respect and you will gain respect.

To have the power is much about having control over the situation. It doesn't mean that you need some sort of absolute control. It means that you delegate and involve other people. If someone has an idea, let them try it and give them some guidelines to go by and set some kind of deadline together. Help them to see the whole picture, so to speak, help them to grow and encourage new ideas.

To be the decision maker doesn't mean that you always have to have the last word. Think about this and have it as a tool because it can be a very efficient tool not to have to be the one who has the last word. It opens things up for discussion. It shows that you listen and really listen and again take it into consideration. When you get input or suggestions for change the company is given a gift. People who come up with suggestions are engaged employees that really want to contribute with their knowledge and experience. This is a good sign when ideas flourish within the company, cheer that on and celebrate your wins together and especially the one or ones who came up with the ideas. Encourage more suggestions in an easy way.

Together with power comes the possibility to recommend others for promotion within the company and to give recommendations. This is also something that calls for you to be really skilled at pin-pointing qualities that other people have. You need to take interest in their qualities and give them the chance to use their skills. To spot employees with qualities is something to really put an effort into, by you as a business leader throughout the company opening up possibilities for promotion and making a career within your company.

When choosing people to promote or to give more

responsibilities to it is important that you analyze why you want to promote this person, what qualities again are at hand here that you want to encourage or reward?

Elitism is a sensitive topic. Who do you choose to promote and why? Is it really possible to get promoted within your company or do you seek it outside the company? If you don't know if you have that competence within the company or you are worried that it will raise some sort of unhealthy competition then you are out of line. Promotion should be possible within the company. You need to develop the skills to spot who to promote and why.

To have development talks with all employees is something that should be documented and is of course classified information. Don't make it too bureaucratic, use a few questions, perhaps just five questions at each meeting. Make them more often and shorter meetings instead of longer meetings, have a good tone, be relaxed and listen to what they have to say. Ask for instance these questions or make your own:

- What do you think is good about working here?
- What do you think is not so good about working here, improvements?
- Are there any conflicts that you think are unsolved or take energy?
- Is there anything that you are worried about that you want to talk about?
- Do you have any suggestions about how to make your job more enjoyable, how would you like to influence your everyday job more?

These are questions that you need to handle to discuss and to encourage employees. To listen has so much power perhaps because it is not so common in our society. To be able to open up and tell their experience at work and privately is a good thing. You get to know your employees and you will get so much in return. You will be part of creating a culture where humans can develop and prosper.

Gather Impressions

Smart is the one that sees the wind of change and adapts to needed circumstances internally and externally.

Influence from Your Team
When a movie is to be recorded there are very strict rules on who does what. Take a look at any casting list at the end of a movie. Actors are cast to different roles with written instructions what to do, how to act and what to say. The one that pays, calls the shots so to speak. The producer pays for the whole project and some sponsors also contribute with the finances. There is not much room for anyone to say, " I think it would be a better ending if we did this another way than the script says." No.

Is your company this strict? It depends on what you are doing and what we are talking about you might say. Be more generous and let people come with their opinion for when it is room for that. Really think through where it is not a good idea for second opinions. Perhaps you will realize that second opinions from the team are very important and will actually improve things and that great teamwork make things so much better. That would perhaps even make a movie better.

The whole idea of a great team is to gather knowledge and get a strong and competent team to lift everything to the very best it can get. Know your strengths and your weaknesses and support the team with people that have the strengths that are needed.

I love the saying that the difference between an A player and a B player is that an A player gets a team together with people that are better, but a B player gets a team that is not as good as him or her because there is a need to feel that you are the best.

To have a so-called helicopter perspective is good. Don't be blindfolded and ignore important signs or opinions. Don't expect others to be blindfolded either. Instead create a culture where opinions and suggestions come freely as contribution to growth, how to improve the company's production and performance on the market. A culture where employees feel that they really can contribute with their opinions and that they make a difference is a workplace where people want to stay and be a part of the company's journey for the long run. To feel that you are a part of creating a company gives motivation to do your very best as an employee.

Influence from Your Customers
It is said that it's ten times more expensive to find a new customer than keep an existing customer. If your company makes a mistake and you deal with the mistake you will build loyalty and even stronger bonds with your customer. That shows that you take responsibility and want to make things right, because you care about what happens to your customer. This also strengthens the sense of responsibility within the company since employees see that you do what is right and think a b o u t long-term relationships with your customers. The employees will also behave this way towards your customers. The opposite behavior, not to take responsibility for your part of the problem will spread this value

within the company and the reputation on the market.

To take your part is important. To take the next step and help out to solve the customer's problems can also be a smart way to do business. Customer relations are important to educate both yourself and your employees with the basics and in depth with those who are in charge of the customers directly. If you are a company that customers feel safe with and you get the reputation that you solve customers' problems and needs, then your company will perform well on the market.

Don't be too dependent on a few customers, spread the risk so to speak and have more customers. You will both learn a lot from different customers' needs and wishes and you will not be so vulnerable. This is something you need to keep as a balance, if you don't have time to take care of the customers you need to make adjustments where you can take resources from within the company. To put down time on customer relations is an investment that will pay off well.

I am much for digitalization of routines and you can save a lot of time to make administration less time consuming. Also contacts with customers can be done efficiently if you have routines where the communication and made agreements are put down into purchase orders thoroughly. There should not be so many emails and there should not be any additional information in emails between different colleagues so you have to read a lot of information from other colleagues. Set up routines with how to approach customers, what to say and how to document it short and close at hand for all who interact with the customers. Good routines save a lot of time and also reduce the risk of misunderstanding and errors.

Customers want to have a swift and smooth contact with your company. You want it to be easy to buy from your company.

It should be a positive experience for the customer to interact with you.

Updates from the Market
The market has changed rapidly in the last ten years, and the market is international more than ever thanks to the digital era. This means new possibilities and new circumstances that not all companies are so familiar with. It means that companies that can easily adapt to changes have advantages compared to companies that don't adapt.

Have the mindset that you need both your customers and your suppliers to do business well. It's a mutual interaction that you need to have in mind. Especially when things get tough on the market you need to be more flexible to both your customers and your suppliers.

We need to understand our customers' conditions on the market if we want to sell more products or services that the they really need. It's leadership to listen and to act towards what is best for the company and its employees, and that includes what the customers need. The market is calling for what they want and your business is to provide the market with what you can contribute with. Henry Ford made this famous comment: – "Our customers can have their car in whatever color they want, as long they want it in black."

A long time ago but a serious mistake that gave the opportunity to General Motors to take a large market share and the competition between Ford started and has continued since then. Not bad for competition because the customers got what they wanted from someone else that listened to them. The lesson is to listen and also adapt to new expectations on the market that you by all means can live up to.

Online business has been around for ten years already. With an international market many buy from other countries instead of at stores at home and businesses are closed. International companies can benefit from large-scale business and bulldoze their way on the international market over small companies.

It is your job as a business leader to decide how to communicate to the market why customers should buy from you. You are responsible for the strategies that you take and not. If you sit back and wait for all to get back to normal what will happen then? Completely new circumstances can become the new normal. Proactive or defensive strategies?

Use the skills and the imagination within your company to identify different possible scenarios, analyze and act if you want to compete on the market. The digital era gives the same possibilities for everyone. Everything can look bigger than it is. Create the feeling that the customers desire to feel and experience.

You can create this online and offline. A small company has the advantage with possibilities to adapt faster than a large company. The problem is that within large companies they have a lot of business skills and they monitor the market more than small companies do but that can change.

If small companies looked over the fence now and then, so to speak, and made adjustments to adapt to what the customers want, they could use their smaller size as an advantage to re-navigate smoother than a large company.

And if small businesses would communicate to the market why they should buy from them, not only with the obvious fact to support your local store or business, then the customers would come back and support your business. Communicate and act towards the customers so they really feel that you care about them and acknowledge their need to feel experiences when they buy things from you that they need and also things they don't need. Create a feeling of want or a hype round your brand.

Influence from Role Models
Our parents, our ancestors, teachers and other adults are our first role models. Unconsciously we get our idea of different leadership styles. When we get older we realize that a good leader doesn't always say yes to everything we want and we might even appreciate some boundaries and what they are good for.

Perhaps we even can understand a bad mood and why and we learn to adapt to expectations to certain behavior first as children and later as adults. We associate accepted behavior with the approval we receive and are eye witnesses to.

We automatically sort behavior as unaccepted behavior when it's sanctioned with some sort of negative consequence. We adapt to behavior and expect others to do the same. We expect consequences to unaccepted behavior and automatically think it is unfair if it doesn't. But we need to be aware that we can adapt to bad behavior. We can even get the wrong idea of certain behavior, like bullying for instance, we might get involved in that and need to be reminded that we have to not take any part in bullying. So-called grown up bullying still exists at work places.

Leadership is closely connected to identity, who we want to be, and that is a good thing because then we can learn to become better and to adapt to modern expectations upon the leadership role. It is important to be a human and not a machine when you deal with other people, we all have feelings and we spend our lives many hours a week at our job. A company is responsible for people's lives at work, and the treatment they are getting themselves exposed to.

This is an important reminder to really have a good leadership style and to help people to prosper within our company where we work. And we also realize that we all influence our work place and this is something that is important to say when we implement the words of value into our companies. And we need to understand the meaning of these words and help others to understand what these words mean in everyday life at work.

We influence each other at work and even customers and suppliers, and the other way around. We interact with other people and exchange influence and we can choose to pick bits and pieces from other people's success into our own performance at work and into our leadership style. We often talk about others; how nice it was to talk to someone on the phone or how rude a person was, it makes us cheerful or upset. This is power that should be used for a good cause and not be manipulative. Your attitude has a great influence at work and it cannot be just a facade because it shows if you are genuine with your traits and efforts or not.

We need to keep adjusting our leadership style to have a modern leadership style. New insights and new expectations are challenges that you can be taught to handle in an effective and genuine way. To say that "I am this way" is not good for anyone. Everything round us is really changing fast and we need to adapt to the changes to have the right competence that is needed for the job as a business leader. The digital era is important to make adjustments towards and to implement into any business and be the role model yourself that changes is needed to have a strong performance on the market and to be a company where both business and people flourish.

To design your leadership style think back on leaders that you have worked with, dos and don'ts, and other people that influenced you in your life, bits and pieces. Write down some traits and situations that you have appreciated and some that you have disliked and why. From this you can mark words that kind of repeat themselves and you will find a guide of words to use as pillars of your leadership style. Save it as **a digital folder of your leadership style** and fill in more insights and situations along the way so you have an updated leadership style that grows with your experience in life and you will too. This will give you a more dynamic view to leadership and you will not lose any insights along the way.

Your Intentions

Areas where you feel challenged or triggered, really analyze where it comes from. Try to view it differently so you turn it into challenges that you enjoy encountering instead of being shaken by an imaginable defeat. You know others will identify this about you so you better be aware of it yourself and learn to master yourself and put out your best version as a business leader. Choose who you want to be and transform into it.

To identify why you want to become a business leader is really a god idea. You have to be aware of your intentions and what drives you towards your goals.

Identify the areas that really give you the motivation and joy to be a business leader. What do you see as obstacles, what triggers you, when do you feel disappointed and why? Identify this so you really get to know yourself well, your strengths and your weaknesses as a leader. Document this in **your leadership folder** for your development.

Useful Personality Traits
I came up with a kind of a philosophical description of a leader, taste these phrases:

Make your intelligence radiate like Cologne. Let your leadership be identified as soulsome

Take interest in your customers like you were their investor. Spice it up with honesty.

Would anyone object to this kind of leadership? Good

intentions, bravery and common sense are rare things these days. You really wonder why. Younger generations are not automatically loyal as previous generations have been. You have to create a culture that makes people grow and thrive if you want them to stay. You can't expect that everyone will stay just because you want them to. Your values show and your colleagues know them very well.

To talk about intentions, you need to use your intelligence for the good of others and for doing business in good faith. To inspire colleagues to work side by side towards goals and the company's vision is really something that should be joyful. To contribute with a source of meaning to be a part of a journey together is important and will create job fulfillment. It will also be easier to understand the big picture. And to really care about your customers will make them stay with your company for the long run and you will be a part of their journey too and see them grow. Honestly, can it even be measured what it costs to do business without honesty and good faith? Think about this in your everyday life at work.

To be the captain of the ship requires different traits depending on different situations and circumstances within a company and how to deal with an ever-changing market. To contribute with a positive view to change and easily communicate the importance of changes, with the aim to adapt to an ever-changing macro environment is crucial. You need to have solid experience within business, you need to be able to make your team contribute with their best efforts.

It is much about being inspirational and courageous to dare to take those decisions that perhaps kind of go against the grain when the territory might feel unknown or uncertain. Before these discussions you need to have gained trust so you use your efforts where they are needed instead of debating what to do and causing demotivation and mistrust.

To help you **cope with uncertainty**, a good idea is to have a digital folder where you keep different assignments organized so you see the topic of it instantly. Don't have too many files, sort them in a logical order so you kind of instantly remind yourself of the uncertainty that was within these projects and the outcome of them. In each project it is a good idea to make a summary in the beginning that pin-points the problem you were facing and the uncertainty, what strategy you used within your team and the outcome, direct outcome and indirect outcome. This is your resumé as a business leader but more detailed and confidential with your gathered experience as your foundation in whatever you will do next.

This will help you to stop wasting time on being uncertain or worried and spreading uncertainty among your employees. Remember that it is not their job to be a support to you if you feel worried. If you get worried say why to show you are a human and then discuss how you together can cope with the challenges at hand. Especially if it is new territory, like during the outbreak of Covid-19, it was something new to everyone, so acknowledge uncertainty and s t a t e that you will cope with it together. But if it is business as usual, you should be the anchor to your employees and support them with trust and encouragement.

To really contribute with progress within leadership is to learn from other leaders' mistakes, within the company but also from the history of leadership. This way your leadership will not go on default because you are designing it and want to make a difference. Time is moving us forward and so should your leadership style. This way you will reach a higher level of leadership. It's an important aspect to be the change towards progress. There is a saying that if you don't move forward you will move backwards. This is applicable within leadership, it moves with time and the market and the society is changing and the leadership style has to fit into the needs of tomorrow and today.

The Company's Vision
There should never be a question of what you are doing and why, within a company, it has to be explained how our priorities fit into the bigger picture, to the vision of the company.

Why we are doing things is a subconscious question that needs to be answered. We all search and make our own conclusions to that question if it isn't logically answered together with the vision we have in our mind. We make up "a why" ourselves so this makes it even more important to have a decided vision of the company. We want to fit into a purpose as to why we are putting down our effort into our everyday job to find job fulfillment.

The company's vision is the direction. You need to visualize the goals along the way to everyone so they understand where you are going together.

The goals along the way are like check points that need to be celebrated together with the teams. We need to have these check points so we all realize that we are on the right track. We need to get the information as a summary of what we really have accomplished together to see that we are making progress. It can drain us of our energy if we only look ahead at how much is left and all the uncertainty that might rise along the way. Therefore, we need to remind ourselves about the journey that we have accomplished already and celebrate that.

This is important if you want to uphold motivation and a sense of purpose within the company among the employees. To have a shared vision towards where we are going has much power. The opposite, to not have a clear vision, raises questions about the leadership and uncertainty within the company's culture.

If the vision is continuously communicated within the company it will be like a compass and you will be the captain of the ship and you will gain trust. Decision making will go easier when you have trust from the employees. They know that you have a plan and they see that you act according to this plan and that you fulfill the goals along the way. You cheer others on and are a team player that enjoys the journey despite perhaps a rocky road. You know what you are doing and you have the company under control. Your purpose as a business leader is to fulfill the company's vision and reach the check points along the way.

To be a team player despite being the business leader is the right way to go. To include others is to listen and gather information from every level within the company. By being present in the everyday workflow you will also take notice about things that happen within the company and you will feel the culture. You will also learn a lot about the everyday work life that the employees have and they will trust you more because you know what you are talking about. This way you will automatically pay attention to what is going on and show interest in the company and the employees. Take tours round the different departments so it is a natural thing to have you everywhere within the company where the action is.

This way you will collect a lot of knowledge about the company and its potential. New ideas will come up o f how to reach the company's vision and new goals along the way thanks to an inspiring and creative culture. This can mean that the vision needs to be adjusted or made bigger because an inspiring culture makes companies grow when people prosper. This will make the company prosper too.

When choosing employees and recommending employees for promotion look for more human signs and a willingness to think outside the box. To try to control people by choosing people that don't have an opinion of their own on the managerial ladder will not help the company to grow and improve its performance on the market. New insights require new thoughts to dare to discuss old habits and come up with new ideas as solutions. Different perspectives are so important and inspiration and creativity need freedom of speech and open minds.

About elitism, it is a wise thing to really consider what this means to you and what to look out for within this area. To only look at static facts of degrees and what school, family or cultural background a person has is something that belongs to the time we have left behind us. Learn instead how to identify intelligence and skills among your employees, know their strengths. Someone's weak spot can be someone else's strength. Build teams by adding strengths to it with people of diversity in skills and personality. Teach the employees this importance by complimenting achievements that individuals have made. When new positions become available write the traits that are needed so people understand that a strong team really needs different skills.

Robots can do the boring parts and we want to use our amazing brain and challenge ourselves, at least if we get to know that this is really possible. Who doesn't want to work within a company where you can be a part of creating a thriving culture and where you feel that you really want to spend your forty hours a week? To be more of a visionary as a business leader is part of your job.